STONEHENGE:
Into the Light
Truth is Stranger Than Fiction

by Mark Zaretti

CW00517286

"STONEHENGE: Into the Light

Truth is Stranger Than Fiction"

by Mark Zaretti

Published by The Way Back Group Ltd: https://thewaybackgroup.org

ISBN 979-8867179175

Books by Mark Zaretti:

The Way Back, The Six Virtues:
A Companion Guide (2019)

STONEHENGE: Into the Light
Truth is Stranger Than Fiction (2023)

Spiritual Life Explained: The Wake-up Call
The Way Back to God (2023)

Each book can be read independently of the others, however they are listed above in the recommended reading order. More books are coming soon and if you would like to be the first to know when they become available please follow the author "Mark Zaretti" on Amazon or "The Way Back" on social media; or sign up to our mailing list via thewaybackgroup.org

Table of Contents

The documentary upon which this book is based

was a massive undertaking aided by the kind

support from a number of people.

Special thanks to Paula, David, S.G.

and all who valued truth.

God bless you all.

Preface

On the surface this book may appear quite far removed from my usual spiritually-focused publications. However there are three important reasons why I produced this book, eventually.

Firstly, spiritual awareness is not confined to just those times when we sit in stillness, rather it can touch every part of life, when we are awake. Spirituality is the backdrop to everything we can possibly explore within our reality, including Stonehenge and our ancient past.

Secondly, "*Truth is TRUTH*" and if you investigate the truth of any topic deep enough, it will eventually bring you to the same fundamental spiritual questions like "*What is life really all about?*".

Thirdly... You will have to wait and see! I promise I will tell you by the end of this book what the third reason was.

Taking into account the first two points though, it means that if we are awake and value truth then there is always benefit to seeking the truth of any subject, even if on the surface it is out of our comfort zone.

So although I am better known as a spiritual teacher guiding people's personal journeys of spiritual awakening and soul-growth, a few years ago my desire for truth led me to uncover fascinating and interwoven information

1

about Stonehenge, the druids, Avebury, the Nazca Lines, pyramids, Atlantis and even the topic of UFOs.

I deliberated for a while on whether to take on this project, but when I realised that this information actually helps explain a lot about the spiritual state of the planet at this time, while also answering some pretty important spiritual questions about the lives we live today, then I eventually decided to share what I had found.

So late in 2022 I started filming a short video, which eventually evolved into a feature-length documentary called "*STONEHENGE: Into the Light*". To this day, this is the single largest media project I have ever undertaken.

One year on and I was compelled to produce this book as a direct transcript of that documentary. This book also has extra scene notes and bonus "*Behind the scenes*" narratives, providing even deeper insights and context.

I have resisted the urge to convert the spoken words from the film's audio into grammatically correct sentences for this book. This means that this book can be read, word for word, alongside the documentary and has the natural feel and flow of a conversation.

The good news is that you do not have to have watched the documentary in order to enjoy this book. Even more good news is that the documentary is available online, completely for free, and there is even an audiobook/

podcast version that you can download too. You will find links to these in the Appendix.

It is said that "*A picture is worth a thousand words*" and I really want you to enjoy reading this book and also get the most from it. So I have lovingly curated key stills from the documentary and inserted these images into the corresponding pages of this book. There are 136 of these images, so I guess that is the equivalent of an extra 136,000 words, bonus!

All joking aside, this book reveals some very important and potentially challenging truths, some of which may at times seem totally "*Out of this world*". This is why it is important to inject a little levity, to remind us all that we are only ever responsible for our reaction to things, not the things themselves.

Therefore, even though what I share may be provoking, I urge you to remain light-hearted and positive. It is actually amazing to realise that it is only because people on the planet are spiritually awakening, that these long-hidden truths, which are stranger than fiction, are finally being brought into the light.

Mark P Zaretti.

Scene 1: Introduction

A SPIRITUAL DOCUMENTARY

STONEHENGE: INTO THE LIGHT

PRESENTED BY MARK ZARETTI MSc

Stonehenge... Forget everything you may have heard.

It is time for the truth.

Spiritual gateway, or something far more sinister?

Was Stonehenge a spiritual portal to another dimension?

Or was it something far more nefarious?

Join me as we explore Stonehenge together...

14TH NOVEMBER 2022, A SUNNY DAY AT STONEHENGE.

Here we are, Stonehenge, probably one of the most famous ancient artefacts shrouded in mystery and superstition.

There's lots of theories about who built it and why:

WE HEAR THE DISTORTED VOICE OF A TOUR GUIDE.

*"...Stonehenge was a national meeting point
4,500 years ago..."*

But these are based on digging in the ground and putting together archaeological evidence.

Chapter 1:   Higher Information?

Is there another source of information that can reveal: Who built it? How was it built? And for what purpose?

These are just some of the questions that I'm going to answer in this documentary, drawing upon higher information that cannot be found in books, and information that up till now has been hidden.

I'm hopefully going to shed light on the mysterious Druids who were involved with the building of Stonehenge.

Who were they? What were they doing here? And importantly I'm going to reveal Stonehenge's role and their role in a much bigger planetary picture, a picture which is literally out of this world.

I'm Mark Zaretti, a spiritual teacher and author. I've got over 40 years of meditation experience including advanced forms of meditation and I've been lucky enough to experience levels of consciousness that are far beyond what we would normally consider the realm of the mind and the physical body.

My pursuit to unravel the bigger picture has taken me in some surprising directions and ultimately it's revealed itself to be the pursuit for the TRUTH.

Sometimes the information that I've gained on the inside has been at odds with what we generally understand from the mainstream education and sciences.

Chapter 2: The Limits of Science

Ultimately I've come to accept that perhaps we can't know everything via the sciences alone and maybe those things that are more mysterious need to be approached in a different way.

I know how difficult it is to reconcile the tangible world with the more spiritual and mysterious one. Although I've been practising meditation most of my life I've also studied biology at university up to the level of a Masters and worked in the biotech and pharmaceutical sectors as well.

Despite my scientific background I've had experiences that simply cannot be explained by science alone so I can appreciate that what I'm about to share with you may challenge some people's concept of the world around them and that's okay because:

"There is never growth without challenging limits."

THERE IS NEVER GROWTH WITHOUT CHALLENGING LIMITS

In 2016 after over 10,000 hours of spiritual meditation I discovered my ability to bring down higher-knowledge. Since then I've been producing podcasts, books, articles, and videos to share what I've learned on the inside with "Seekers of Truth".

Chapter 3: Seekers of Truth

Time and again the information I found on the inside has been proven to be true, sometimes years later.

Such spiritual knowledge is higher than anything we can gain with our senses down here on the third dimension and as a spiritual teacher and a sharer of information I've decided that:

"I will always speak the truth."

Understandably speaking the truth, especially speaking about spiritual truth has provoked quite a few people, particularly those that do not want you to know the truth. But I decided that:

> "It is better to stand for the truth,
> than to fall for deception."

And so I promise you I am going to speak openly, honestly, and share all that I have learned about Stonehenge and the Druids. I do not want you to believe me, instead use this information as a starting point for your own exploration, perhaps you'll discover even more. The good thing about the TRUTH is that:

> "Eventually the truth will always come out."

My focus is spiritual and I've got to be honest, I've never really been interested in such worldly affairs as Stonehenge, or the Great Pyramids, or the Nazca Lines, and things like this. But in the research for my latest book I discovered a shocking connection between the Druids of Stonehenge and a group of beings on higher dimensions who have been involved in the affairs of Earth for a very long time.

So to help explain what I've discovered I've driven all the way here to Stonehenge to explore more and to share with you on this journey:

- *Who were The Druids?*

- *How did they build Stonehenge?*

- *What did they build it for?*

- *And is there a connection between Stonehenge, the Nazca Lines, and Avebury?*

10

Scene 2: Stonehenge's Origins

Stonehenge is in fact much older than we believe or understand.

The original henge, which consists of the perimeter ditch and raised ground was originally built approximately 9,700 BC. This included the Z and Y holes and the Aubrey holes, which had posts in them.

Now what is clear even today is that these posts and the holes allowed those people at the time to predict exactly when the summer and winter solstices would be.

Chapter 4: A Giant Year Clock

In effect the original henge was a year clock so that they could accurately know, to the day, when certain alignments were going to happen.

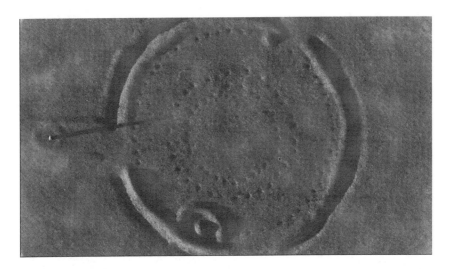

Knowing this leads to an understanding of the original purpose of the henge. I say the "Original purpose" because its purpose changed over time.

What we need to ask ourselves is: "Why would someone thousands of years ago need to know the exact day of the year?"

When we consider life on Earth on this physical plane, it's governed by basic needs especially if we think back thousands of years to what it must have been like then.

Warmth, shelter, security, food.

When it comes to knowing what time of year it is, this really relates to agriculture. But early man would have been able to know when to sow seeds and when to reap the harvest.

As the plants start to rise in spring there would be clues, when the leaves start to fall off the trees in autumn there is the clue that winter is coming.

In other words the reason for this year clock could not possibly have been for agriculture it's far too accurate. They would have had enough clues from nature alone to determine when to grow the plants and when to harvest them.

To understand why they needed this year clock, and remember we're talking before the stones even existed, think about modern times. What is it that necessitates us knowing exactly what time it is? What day of the week it is? What month? Etcetera.

If we did away with the calendar and clocks we would still eat, we would still have shelter, we would still survive and thrive.

13

The main reason we today have calendars and apps on our phones and things like this is to make sure that we're on time, specifically for meetings with others.

Or in the case of airports and transport, to be there when something departs or when something arrives. This is the reason why we have this quite staggering year clock. It's to allow people back then to be present at important meetings.

Chapter 5: The Leader

The group who first established this henge and built the year clock were asked to do so by their leader. And it is because of this leader that my attention was drawn to Stonehenge.

The name of this leader became known to me several years ago and the group who established this monument behind me, known as "Druids" are named after him.

So when I learned of his name it drew my attention to the Druids and that is why I'm here today.

Not because I was interested in Stonehenge but because I discovered who the leader is of the Druids.

Now if we were to go back 11,700 years then the word "Druid" would be more accurately pronounced "D#####'s" in homage to the name of this leader.

Although I pronounced the old name for the Druids in the video, I deliberately obfuscated it slightly so as not to reveal the name of their leader, hence also why I've put #s above. In time his name will be revealed but this is not the book for that, and now is not the time for that either. This story is part of a much bigger picture and as you read on you will understand why such matters must be approached with caution.

And the reason he asked them to build this was so that he could come down and visit with them twice a year to give them instructions and guidance to carry out his will on the third dimension.

This leader who the Druids were named after is ancient. In fact he's older than humanity as you know them, and he's far older than what we recognise around us as this physical plane. Indeed far older than Stonehenge and the Druids themselves. And despite being ancient, he's not all-knowing, he's not all powerful, and he's not benevolent. This leader does not have humanity's best interests in mind.

I have not named him in this documentary and his name has never appeared in any of the ancient texts. There is hardly any reference to him and you would not notice it if you saw it unless you knew.

But his allies who have helped him govern this, are well known and some of their names may be familiar to you including Pan, Lilith, and Satan. This should leave you in no doubt as to his malevolence.

DRAMATIC DRUM BEATS AND A MONTAGE OF LEAVING STONEHENGE AND DRIVING TO A NEARBY LOCATION.

Scene 3: Beyond the Perimeter

So I've moved away from Stonehenge. I've come down this country lane that runs almost to the entrance to Stonehenge and I've got a perfect view, I'm looking at it dead ahead of me now.

Outside of the perimeter of Stonehenge it's much easier to talk freely. There were so many tourists in there and guides and people milling about that it's very difficult to speak about these matters without kind of drawing attention. And that's why I've chosen to come away from Stonehenge a little bit. And this way I can talk more freely so that I can speak the truth and tell you more about what I've learnt.

Chapter 6: Dark Meetings

"The Leader", as the Druids knew him, they didn't know where he was from, they believed he was from the stars. But he was

actually on a higher dimension of Earth, and he would descend down to them to guide them twice a year at the winter and summer solstice, which is why they needed the year clock.

He did this using what seems like very advanced technology to us but was actually quite ancient technology to him, and he also used black magic.

And the reason is that this technology and the ability to shift between dimensions isn't natural, and the the black magic was needed in order to provide power and fuel for this interdimensional tunnel.

The Druids would gather at the henge and where the Slaughter Stone is. So you have the Heel Stone and then the Slaughter Stone which kind of marks the gateway into the henge.

The Slaughter Stone is so named because in ancient times in the Stone Age they noticed that there's a lot of iron ore in that particular stone and so it rusts and appears to have blood.

But the truth is that in the vicinity of that stone at the entrance to the henge these Druids would perform dark and black magic rituals, slaughtering animals in order to generate a lot of ungodly and negative energy to correlate with the negative energy that The Leader was using to create this tunnel.

Chapter 7: Interdimensional Tunnels

And so The Leader would manifest this tunnel using his dark magic and the Druids would contribute with the dark energy produced from the black magic that they were doing and the ritualistic slaughter of life, and the tunnel would open at the actual entrance by the slaughter stone and The Leader would walk out.

And he would appear to them, physical, so though he came from higher dimensions where he was non-physical the process of coming down the tunnel would allow him to manifest into physical form albeit not for a long period of time, but long enough to meet with the Druids.

Now these meetings were obviously very important and were fundamentally about him giving the Druids instructions on how they can manipulate and control life on the third dimension.

They didn't all live locally and they came from different places to be here for this meeting and he would instruct them on things like which families to trust; which to kill; where to conquer; where to attack; what to do in terms of planning for the future; organisations to create, secret or otherwise.

It was about him using the Druids to consolidate his grip upon the third dimension and ultimately upon humanity, you and I.

So this was the boss coming down to tell his management layer, "Right, this is what you need to do", and it was strategy, and it was planning, and it was all done in the shadows.

Now he didn't always come himself, he wasn't just ruling the third dimension. This leader is actually the leader of much more than you or I could be aware of. And so sometimes he would send those closest to him in his stead.

And one of those characters that he would send down was someone that goes by the name of Pan, although they have gone by many other names.

Chapter 8: Introducing Pan

And this is why Pan worship, which is the roots of Paganism, arose amongst the Druids, because they recognized that this individual was very very close to The Leader.

And this individual, as they have done on many occasions when they have come down to the third dimension under other identities, beguiled them and led them to believe that he was so important.

The truth is that Pan is actually the son of this leader and that's why he was so trusted that he would come in his stead to rule over the kingdom of the third dimension plane, what we call Earth, what we call home.

And as an aside you may want to consider the word "Pandemonium" or "Pan-DEMON", again it lends to the fact that these beings or people were not coming down here for good reasons.

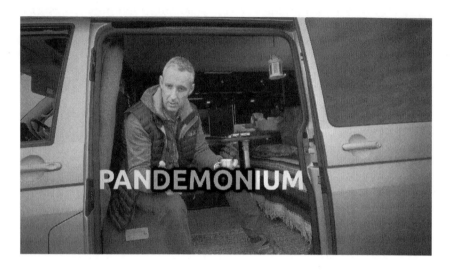

They were not looking out for humanity, they came to control.

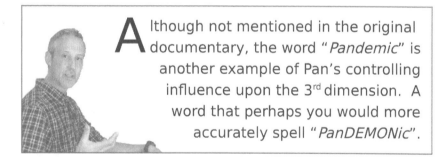

Although not mentioned in the original documentary, the word "*Pandemic*" is another example of Pan's controlling influence upon the 3rd dimension. A word that perhaps you would more accurately spell "*PanDEMONic*".

So we're going to take a walk and see if we can go further around to the other side.

Scene 4: Next to Stonehenge

Okay so the question is who were these Druids? They were actually a council of twelve representing the twelve different races that were aligned with The Leader.

Chapter 9: Stellaglyphs

It may be hard to comprehend but the different animals represented in the constellations are actually stellaglyphs, glyphs made out of stars representing these different races.

For example serpents, beers, and lizards. And these twelve races that formed the "Council of Druids" are amongst those

25

represented by these stellaglyphs. These glyphs represent all the different races that have an interest in the third dimension plane.

So have you ever wondered why it is that the same animal glyphs and symbols that are featured in the constellations are also repeated, for example, in the Nazca Lines and in petroglyphs around the world.

Chapter 10:   Ancient Races

Most ancient races and indigenous tribes often have in their ancestry story folklore references to mythical animals or almost god-like animalistic beings that are either their founders or played an important role in the establishment of their tribes

For example the serpents of Australia and the wolves of Rome.

Perhaps it's easiest to understand these stellaglyphs or petroglyphs in terms of them being flags marking territory. So for example wherever you find the the serpent either built into rocks, or in the Nazca Lines, or in the constellations in the night sky, this is marking that particular territory as "This belongs to the serpents".

Now three of the members of the Druid council actually belonged to a similar root race and these three races were all much more technologically advanced than the others in the group. But since they were in an alliance they shared their technology. And it was this technology that was used eventually in the formation of Stonehenge.

Chapter 11:   The Egyptian Connection

These three races actually went on to form the major civilizations in Egypt and Mesopotamia.

And that's why there as well you see these megalithic ancient structures that quite frankly belie belief as to how they were constructed. But they used the same technology and the same techniques as was being refined here.

So you may wonder why these three races were so technologically and scientifically advanced, and to answer that you actually have to go back to BC 16,000.

At that time one of these races came down to what we call Earth, the physical plane, and established five research sites, two of which are extremely well known.

One of them perhaps you've heard of was Atlantis, the other one was Hy-Brasil.

Now there they developed technology over thousands of years that by our standards is way advanced of anything that we know in the mainstream.

It was actually the leader of that race on higher dimensions who destroyed Atlantis and sunk it into the ocean.

He did so because he was outraged that his researchers that he'd sent down from higher dimensions to the physical plane were sharing some of the knowledge of their technology with the humans that were there. And so he, in a fit of rage, wiped out Atlantis and killed off pretty much all of the humans there.

*Now he did this by using his power on higher dimensions to manifest what appeared to be a natural disaster on the physical plane. Now **this isn't the only time** this has ever happened, and there are quite ancient disaster stories that are well documented about floods for example, where such "Apparently" natural phenomena have actually been instigated from higher dimensions.*

Maybe it is easier to contemplate such inter-dimensional meddling in the distant past, which seems so detached from the lives we live today. But I draw your attention to the fact I said "*This isn't the only time*". Reflect upon the many "Apparently" natural disasters in current times. Could there be a connection?

A few of the researchers at that site were forewarned of what was going to happen and managed to escape taking with them the knowledge of the technology that they had developed.

Chapter 12:   Ancient Technology

So they actually escaped in what would best be described as "Flying craft". But these craft could not only fly but they had the

29

ability, based on technology that they... that they had developed while on the physical plane, they had the technology to raise in vibration.

And so they were able to not only escape the disaster on the third dimension but return to their original dimension, which is a much higher dimension.

And this is how this technology that was developed 16,000 BC was able to be used in the construction of Stonehenge. Because those races were now allied with The Leader.

One of the technologies they had learned and were now able to share was the creation of interdimensional tunnels.

There's so much more that could be said about Atlantis and Hy-Brasil and what happened, and in the book I do go into a lot more detail, but the problem is that Hy-Brasil and Atlantis are no longer present for us to study and to observe.

And so they could be dismissed simply as fanciful imagination or fairy tale. But when you have something like Stonehenge that actually physically exists and dates back thousands of years, then what you have is irrefutable proof of something.

And what Stonehenge really represents is a crossover point between the reality that we understand down here as "The third dimension and the physical plane", and a vaster reality that's happening even now on higher dimensions.

And this is a pinch-point if you like, where at some point at least in the past, the two have crossed.

Chapter 13:   Life on Higher Dimensions

Even if the concept and idea of life and existence on higher dimensions that are beyond most people's awareness is too hard to swallow, is too big a leap for... for people, these giant stones that weigh over 25 tons and similarly the Great Pyramids of Giza, and the stone walls of interlocking perfectly engineered stones at Sacsayhuaman in Peru, all point to some greater mystery.

Mark Zaretti - 2011
Sacsayhuaman, Peru

The mainstream theories about how these things were crafted and built seem woefully inadequate. So Stonehenge, like other ancient relics, point to the fact that there are perhaps mysteries that are beyond the explanation of the mundane and the everyday.

That perhaps the mainstream is not able to answer, and if nothing, just the sheer size and the presence of such a phenomena on the planet inspires some kind of deeper enquiry into what is going on.

And so while it is easy to dismiss Atlantis and Hy-Brasil, we cannot dismiss Stonehenge because it is there, present, and tangible, leaving the door open to a deeper enquiry.

So going back to a time when the henge was first created, before the big stones were put in, this whole land would have been surrounded by lush woodlands and the small stakes and smaller standing stones would not have been visible. In fact it would have all been obscured.

Chapter 14:   Arriving at the Henge

So when I first arrived a couple of days ago at the Stonehenge campsite I wanted to experience what it might have been like for people thousands of years ago to come across this giant construction. And so I walked from the campsite for several hours through fields and across footpaths and bridleways.

And it was only when I was maybe a mile away, just to the south, that I could actually see it and it was small.

And furthermore because the path undulated up and down when I carried on it disappeared from view again, and if you take into account the trees that would have been there, what it it suggests is that this structure was not built as a gathering place, a "Beacon for humanity", to gather in celebration.

Anyone capable of stacking stones like that could have easily have created something much higher than the surrounding trees. They could have chosen a location that was easier to see; they could have lit a fire on top. But there's no evidence of any of that so clearly this was something built for a purpose that was not for the masses. Stonehenge was for its Druid keepers and its leader and it was a secret site.

Chapter 15:   700 Years

For the next 700 years The Leader and the council on the third dimension would meet twice a year at the solstices. He would give them instruction and they would follow.

Obviously those down here would not live as long as him and so they would pass on the title to the next one in their bloodline, if he approved. And so their secret ways, their teachings, their black magic, and their Druid lore was passed on down the bloodlines and the tradition of the Druids and the purpose of meeting with The Leader was preserved.

Now this went on for 700 years and that may seem like a long time but to The Leader it is nothing and so for 700 years he would come down and rule over this council and they in turn would rule over the lands that they controlled.

There was so much more I wished to share with you but heavy rain came down forcing me to stop. I was however able to capture this moody sunset time-lapse since my GoPro was waterproof. But with a tight schedule and even more heavy rain predicted for the following day it seemed our window for filming at Stonehenge was over.

Scene 5: Breakfast Reflections

15TH NOVEMBER 2022. WE FIND OURSELVES IN MARK'S CAMPERVAN ON A VERY WET AND WINDY MORNING AS HE PREPARES BREAKFAST.

Good morning. So I'm just sorting out breakfast; it's a particularly wet and wild day today and yesterday we were at Stonehenge.

The plan for today, I've just been checking the map on my phone, is to go up to Avebury. I've also been looking at the weather and it doesn't look good, but we will not be deterred.

I wasn't going to say anything about this really, this isn't something I intended to discuss in this documentary but I think it is highly relevant.

I film on a GoPro just a really simple easy to use camera, practically bomb-proof. I mean these things get attached to motorbikes and BMXs and thrown down the side of mountains. They're waterproof, they're drop proof, and there's really just one button: Start recording, stop recording. And I've used the GoPro I have for quite some time, kept in very good condition, and I know it well. And I have a very basic audio recording device.

Chapter 16:   Dark Suppression?

Yesterday I started introducing some rather unsavoury characters, The Leader, original Druids, and the ones on higher dimensions that they're all aligned with.

And I also talked about things like black magic, and the use of black magic to allow these characters to move between dimensions. Maybe this is getting ahead of ourselves in this

documentary but it's relevant and I'll mention it now. This still goes on to this day.

Now what I found is when I talk to camera, I've done a lot of videos and I've done a lot of public presentation, and it comes easy. I normally know what I want to say and it comes out without lots of pausing and kind of brain fog.

Well when I arrived at Stonehenge yesterday, in the morning, it was nice and clear there was no one there and it was very misty, but beautiful.

WE JUMP BACK IN TIME TO FOOTAGE FILMED EARLY
YESTERDAY MORNING ON MARK'S PHONE.

"So here I am at the Stonehenge I've arrived quite early and you can just see it there in the background and it's a very misty day."

I had to wait till 9:30 till the park opens and then I moved my van round to the public... kind of the main car park, paid my money and came in with the camera equipment.

When I first arrived at the Stonehenge visitor's centre to get a ticket I had my professional camera tripod on me. I was told I would not be allowed to enter with the filming equipment, so I had to return to my van and leave behind a lot of the equipment, including the tripod. I only took in a clip-on-mic and my GoPro on a tiny hand-held tripod, which is why many of the opening shots were hand-held. Those few shots within the grounds of Stonehenge where the camera was static were achieved by resting the camera atop a fence post or on my rucksack on the ground.

From that moment forwards I really really struggled. It was like there was some kind of uh... an oppressive presence or force trying to give me brain fog. And so I really had to, kind of, keep going back to my notes, which is not like me at all.

When I look back at the footage I'm thinking "Yeah, the stuff I said is all relevant, but the, the way I was talking was very kind of staccato and very suppressed".

But what really clinched it for me was that I actually had to stop recording. When I said yesterday that I left the park because there were too many people and I wanted to take a step back and be more free to speak that's true. But there was another reason.

Chapter 17:   Electronics Going Wrong

The camera itself was just locking up, it was not behaving. It wouldn't stop recording; it wouldn't start recording; when I had stopped it I couldn't start it again. I changed the batteries; I switched it off, reset it.

It was like it was being interfered with and the word "Interference" in the work I do... this comes up a lot and it's a way of referring to "When a person or an object is being messed with by things unseen".

And you could label it as "Magic", or "Spells", or "Palls", or "Hexes", or "Black magic", or any of these things. But really it just means that, in some way something intangible, something that we can't necessarily understand on the physical, is being done to mess with said person or object.

So I left Stonehenge, came back to the van, and in the peace and quiet of my van I was able to, in the same way I get information that I'm sharing with you in this documentary, I was able to find out what had been done and remove these blocks and these, let's just call them "Curses", upon the equipment. And then the GoPro started working fine.

What is noteworthy is that I've used the GoPro camera many times in the twelve months since then and it has never repeated the problems I experienced back on that day.

And since I've been here I've noticed... I mean some lights in the van will start flashing inexplicably, and things like this.

Actual footage

NB: All lights in the van are on a single master switch. Each light is independantly switched by touching its metal surround. It should be impossible for that light to switch on and off while the other lights remain on without being physically touched.

I was out walking the dog in the, in the night, because I sometimes like to, you know, just before going to bed give the dog a walk and stretch both of our legs.

I heard something whoosh over my head probably only two or three meters above but it didn't sound like a drone it didn't sound like a craft that I recognise, it didn't sound like an animal.

It had a very unusual almost electrical sound to it. Now I've got no idea what it was I couldn't see anything, it was a clear night sky. I've never experienced that before.

Chapter 18: Speaking the Truth

There's definitely something going on here. Whatever it is, it seems to be that "They" do not want this video to be made, which just spurs me on even more.

So whether the weather is seemingly against us or whether there are forces seemingly against us, I am absolutely devoted to speaking the truth, and I will not be stopped from speaking the truth.

I know some of this maybe sounds completely crazy. You know if I'd heard myself speaking these things or someone else say talking like this years ago I probably would have dismissed them as a wack.

And I think that's partly how we've been conditioned to think about people that speak up about things that are maybe not mainstream, is we're too quick perhaps to label them as either a "Wacko" or a "Conspiracy theorist".

But if you'd walked the journey that I've walked over the last 20 plus years you'd probably be sitting in this seat saying the same things that I am.

We need to open our minds, we need to... maybe "Mind" isn't the right word actually there, but we need to be more conscious and perhaps less reactive.

But it's in that stillness of observing rather than reacting in terms of intellect, and habit, and thought, and prejudice, and all of these things ...

> *"But it's in that stillness where we can have an enquiry into the nature of things."*

Chapter 19:   Avebury Plans

So the plan for today is we're going to go up to Avebury and we're going to look at the stones there. Which I can tell you now it's going to be... it's quite interesting why they're there, what their purpose was, and it ties in with Stonehenge.

As I said and as you've seen on my sat nav the plan was indeed to head straight to Avebury as time was limited.

WE WATCH THE CAMPERVAN LEAVE THE CAMPSITE AS HEAVY RAIN POURS DOWN.

But as I left the campsite though it was still raining I saw this amazing rainbow, ignoring the weather forecast which was the non-stop rain I followed my intuition and instead of heading to Avebury I went in the other direction back to Stonehenge.

Though it was very cold, sure enough as I arrived the sun broke through the clouds providing an unexpected chance to share with you what the rain had prevented the day before.

Scene 6: Stonehenge Revisited #1

Okay we've had a fortunate break in the weather so I've returned to Stonehenge and you can just see it's way off in the distance there.

It's actually less than half a kilometre but it gives you an idea of how small it really is in the grand scheme of things.

Chapter 20:   Megalithic Constructions

Why after 700 years of using the year clock to organize and coordinate their biannual meetings with The Leader, why did the Druids then place these megalithic stones in the ground? What had changed?

A ccuracy and authenticity is vitally important to me. So when it came to creating the 3D models of Stonehenge I started from scratch. I obtained an archaeological aerial diagram of the Stonehenge site and used this as the basis for my 3D models. This means the position and scale of every single stone, post, mound, henge and ditch is as precise as I could make it.

Well in order to answer this you need to understand that the council on the third dimension, these twelve Druids that govern different lands and would congregate here twice a year, was part of a much bigger chain of command.

Chapter 21:   Higher Councils

In fact it's the... these twelve were the lowest rung of the ladder. There is another council of twelve on a much higher dimension and even higher up than them is another council of twelve and above them a third council of twelve. So this was the lowest of four rungs and above all of them is The Leader.

Affairs on Earth had evolved quite considerably. There was much more interest in humanity as things were evolving and in the third dimension and so The Leader was increasingly having to give his attention on higher dimensions to govern things there as well.

And with this chain of command, although the third dimension and humanity were the primary focus of his manipulation and control, he needed to delegate.

Now with the exception of Pan and one or two others who he really trusted because they were either directly in his bloodline or had proven their loyalty, he didn't want to give the technology that he used on himself and allowed Pan to use to those others.

This technology, that he used, allowed him in person without the aid of craft or anything, via black magic, to come down via these interdimensional tunnels. That's extremely powerful technology so he wasn't about to hand it over to people that he didn't trust so well.

So he said to his generals and those that were going to start governing the third dimension in his stead: "If you're going to go down there you'll do it my way. You're not going to have this personal technology, you're going to use craft."

And he turned to those three races who were represented by some of the Druids down here, who were the extremely technologically advanced ones having also been involved with Atlantis and he leveraged his alliance with them to gain access to their flying craft technology.

And so it's actually the craft that were used to escape from the destruction of Atlantis circa 12,000 BC, that were actually employed to bring his delegates down to this site so that they

could run the biannual meetings and help govern the third dimension with the Druid council.

So what we're looking at when we look at Stonehenge is actually an interdimensional airport, and the stones were necessary infrastructure to support the arrival and departure of these interdimensional craft.

Chapter 22:   Building Stonehenge

So how did they construct this? This is one of the biggest points of speculation. Did they drag these twenty-six ton stones on rollers across undulating fields and through woods? It seems far-fetched really.

Now this stone part of the construction was done about 9,000 BC much earlier than actually is believed when you go through the

tourist place and they show you the timelines, Stonehenge seems much much younger than that.

Therefore at 9,000 years BC it predates the pyramids, it predates the Sacsayhuaman stone walls, and all the other megalithic structures, and what we're actually looking at is the precursor to all of those structures.

Chapter 23: Moving the Stones

The technology that they use to cut these stones and move these stones would go on to be used to do the Egyptian pyramids among other things.

And remember it's the same Druids, the same races involved who were in Atlantis who lent their technology to provide the craft to come down to Stonehenge, who would then go on to establish the Egyptian pyramids.

So there is this connection between all of these different myths, legends and things that are physically tangible.

The technology they actually used were these devices which they would attach to a rock. And then once they activated it, it would cause it to vibrate and shift in vibration until it levitated and then it could just be pushed along.

But in order to activate them it required a lot of energy and not the kind of energy that you would normally find in nature. And so they used black magic to draw down really dark and evil energy from higher dimensions as well as to produce it there and focus it into these devices.

And so just as the interdimensional tunnels were technology-based, they were also black magic-based. And when we talk about black magic what we're really talking about is very very evil and dark and this is really why a lot of the lore and legend of magic associated with Stonehenge should really be approached with caution.

Because all magic ultimately is an attempt to interfere with, or go against nature.

So there weren't hordes of horses and men and rollers and all of these things. It was very very simple, but before they could move these boulders they had to cut them.

They didn't just find all of these perfectly rectangular boulders and when you look closely at these rocks they've got tongue-and-groove joints, they've got pegs, they've got holes.

All of these features were hewn from the rock using another device. It was similar technology. Again, it worked on sound vibrations. You had this device that you attached to a hard stone.

Carve this hard stone in the usual way using hand tools to make a sharp blade and then you would attach this resonating device to it and it would cause it to vibrate and those vibrations would allow it to cut through stone almost as easy as a knife through butter.

And so that's how they were able to shape all these stones with ease and then once they cut them they could then levitate them and just push them along to arrive at their destination.

And this is exactly how the Egyptian pyramids were built.

With the Egyptian pyramids they were travelling over sand a lot of the time so they had to pour water down to solidify the sand but it was really quite straightforward.

Now to us this seems like ridiculously-advanced technology but life on higher dimensions is ancient and so they were doing this 12,000 years, 14,000 years BC in Atlantis. And this is why we can't understand or we speculate that they carved these rocks using bronze tools and dragged them across the ground.

I don't know which is more far-fetched the idea that there might be more to life than just this and that there may be ancient technologies, which are after all depicted in petroglyphs and hieroglyphs across the world. Or that somehow people managed to drag these rocks tens or hundreds of miles using just brawn and rough rope. You decide.

Chapter 24:   The Purpose of Stonehenge

So why have they built the infrastructure the way it is?

You have a circle of sarsen stones and then within that you have the trilathons which are the taller sarsen stones with the caps across the top. The sarsen stone circle itself had the cap stones as well.

Now these two parts are the key infrastructure to do with bringing in the craft and allowing the craft to leave. But they also still needed a way of tracking the day so that they knew when the meetings would be.

And at this point with these big stones in place the Aubrey holes and the Y and Z holes and posts were quite outdated and harder to spot because of all these other stone structures. And so what they then put in place was the blue stones to act as the markers for the year clock. They'd upgraded their system.

They then started using the North and South barrows as elevated posts from which they could act as sentries to make sure that no one was in the stone circle when it needed to be used. And also to get a better view because once they'd elevated the... the site using Stones they needed to have points of elevation from which they could perceive with ease.

Chapter 25:   Why the Stone Horseshoe?

So why this open horseshoe, open into alignment with the Heel Stone and then the surrounding ring which is slightly lower? It doesn't make sense when you look at it from the ground but imagine coming in on a craft down The Avenue in the direct line with the Heel Stone into the horseshoe.

The horseshoe is elevated and it's to do with the trajectory of the craft. These craft didn't "Drop down", they "Came in", because they came from higher dimensions, swung around as they dropped in vibration and then came on a very specific trajectory as they exited the wormhole over the Heel Stone and in to the horseshoe.

And so they had to be able to fly over the outer ring of stones and come into the horseshoe to rest, which is why the outer stones are lower than the horseshoe.

But there's something really important that we need to understand. If you bring energy from a higher dimension down to the third dimension it's dangerous. It's a much higher-vibration, it's much more kind of potent, it's not meant to be here.

Chapter 26:   Harmful Energy

Now we experience that kind of energy occasionally and it is basically radiation, although often it's made by using technology on the third dimension to release energy that is not meant to be experienced on the third dimension. And that's when we have very kind of harmful forms of radiation.

But when these craft come down they're using higher-dimensional energy just as the black magic that the Druids were using to draw down ungodly energy.

Now not all higher-dimensional energy is bad the... there's a lot of good, but it's not meant to be down here, you're not meant to bring that energy down.

In the case of the craft though the energy they were using was bad as well so it's even worse and so when the craft arrived it would bring with it almost like an aura of higher-dimensional energy and it would also be using ungodly energy as its form of propulsion.

Chapter 27:   Why the Stone Outer Ring?

And this explains why we have the outer ring of stones. That is a protective shield to protect the Druids who were waiting for the arrival of The Leader, or The Leader's envoy, from this radiation.

Under the guidance of The Leader they had imbued that outer ring with black magic to form a domed perimeter of energy lines made out of dark energy and what that did is it contained all of that radiation.

If they hadn't done that they would have been burnt much like someone that say has been out in the sun for too long and they literally get sunburnt.

As an aside you may want to ponder: "Why is it that if we evolved, supposedly, on this planet, under that sun, why does it burn us if we get exposed to it too much?" That's worth considering. But that's way beyond the scope of this particular documentary, but I will be explaining it in the books.

But coming back to this. The outer ring is a protective field so that the radiation of the craft does not leak out and harm the

Druids and anyone else there, all of whom were bad, but they still don't want to harm them because they were in alliance with the people coming down.

Chapter 28:   The Energy to Leave

Now once the craft was down eventually it would have to leave. Just as landing uses less energy than taking off in an aeroplane, it needed a lot of energy to get from the third dimension, off the ground, and back to the higher dimensions, and this is the reason for the inner horseshoe.

It's not just there to kind of act as a marker for where to land. It was also imbued with dark magic and energy grids around it so that it could be used by the occupants of the craft when they were ready to leave.

They would get back into their craft when it was time to go and they would invoke powerful dark magic to draw down demonic-ungodly-energy from a massive reserve that they had created on higher dimensions.

And this energy would stream into this horseshoe and be contained by the field setup by these energy grids, and the craft would draw it in to power itself so that it could then leave and return to the higher dimensions.

Now this is really ungodly energy, very nasty stuff, and the stones would contain it and when the craft had gone any residual radiation, any residual ungodly energy, would be absorbed into the stones and into the ground, and most of it would eventually dissipate.

This is one of the reasons... what we've got to understand is, these races that were here to manipulate humanity; to control humanity; subdue us; to keep us in the dark; they weren't good.

But all of this bad energy that would accumulate, partly through their black magic and through the arrival of the craft, was actually nourishing to them because they themselves were bad.

What they were doing was bad. So for them the kind of residual energy that would permeate the ground and radiate outwards was actually supportive.

The negativity made them feel good and this is one of the reasons why there's this idea about the "Healing properties of Stonehenge".

At each solstice The Leader would send lots of dark energy down to Stonehenge because he knew that his servants, those that he was controlling, those who were doing his work, would gather there.

And this energy, it was like just, just how you feel when perhaps you go on holiday and you're by a waterfall and it's like "Oh this is beautiful and uplifting", for them being dark, this outpouring of dark energy upon that place was healing and cathartic.

And the healing for them was real because those who have turned away from the light cannot be healed by the light but they could get nourishment and feel revitalised and their bodies, which are the lowest part of them, would also benefit.

This reservoir of ungodly energy on higher dimensions was actually managed and maintained by one of the higher-councils because they were collaborating with what was happening on the third dimension, so they would know that there were craft coming they would know when to build up the energy reserves to allow this kind of interdimensional transportation.

Now just to give you an idea of how different these craft are to what we're familiar with like flying aeroplanes, and helicopters, and balloons and stuff like this. To get from the higher dimension where they left and to arrive here was about a two minute journey, and it's really understandable why people might think of these things as "UFOs".

Chapter 29:   UFOs?

I'm going to talk about how their propulsion systems actually worked and how they jumped between dimensions, but they were disc-shaped the archetypal original idea of a UFO was a saucer or a disc.

But they were not UFOs. They were interdimensional-craft, coming from Earth on a higher dimension to Earth on a lower dimension.

The idea that we are one of many many planets floating through space being visited by UFOs from other planets, and other galaxies, and other systems has been deliberately encouraged and propagated to hide the truth.

These aren't visitors from another planet, these are visitors from this planet. But if people understood that, if people knew about higher dimensions, then they would start to enquire in that way and the truth would become known.

But The Leader and his councils do not want humanity to know the truth. So to cover up any awareness of these craft, the idea that these craft come from other planets has been propagated.

"The UFO ideology is a huge distraction."

They're not visitors from another planet, but if everyone's looking out across the heavens to other planets and no one's looking up at what's happening on this planet then we'll all stay in the dark.

And so this is why the UFO arena, which is fascinating, is becoming so mainstream and so... if you like, it's another hoax, it's another "Smoke and mirrors".

I cannot stress the point made above enough. It is not suggesting that people are not witnessing "UFOs". However it is important to understand that the notion UFOs come from another physical planet is a deliberate deception, to keep you unaware of the much bigger picture. Part of this dark deceit is to make us feel insignificant, like a speck of dust amidst a vast cosmos. But nothing could be further from the truth! As I have already hinted: Earth matters, YOU matter, and the whole mainstream UFO agenda is another facet of a controlling deception.

So going back 9,000 BC, interdimensional craft from higher dimensions of Earth started landing here, bringing envoys of The Leader to teach, lead, and guide the council on the third dimension.

So why were they saucer shaped? This is all to do with the form of interdimensional-shifting they used.

Within each of these craft, in the very centre, was a "Vortex generator". And what energy vortexes do, which is very similar if you know anything about energy systems in your own body. If you know about chakras, they take energy from higher-vibrations and they slow it down to drop it in vibration or they can speed it up to raise it in vibration.

So on higher dimensions they would activate the downward vortex and take off, rapidly they would drop in vibration and as they arrived at Stonehenge they would have shifted the vibration of the craft and the occupants to what I call "Pseudo-physical".

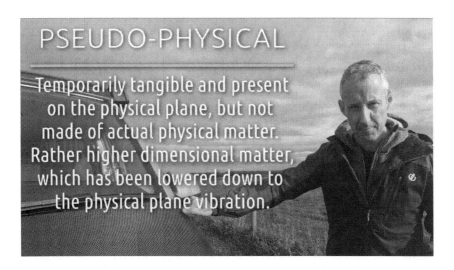

PSEUDO-PHYSICAL

Temporarily tangible and present
on the physical plane, but not
made of actual physical matter.
Rather higher dimensional matter,
which has been lowered down to
the physical plane vibration.

They would be at the same vibration, for example as this van, but they wouldn't be permanently physical, it would be a

67

temporary sort of physicality. But it was enough that they could interact with the people on the third dimension and interact with the environment around them.

And when they were ready to go they would flick the vortex to the upward vortex and that would rapidly raise the vibration of them and the craft they're in, shifting them.

And at the same time they would take off and leave and by time they were over the Heel Stone and out of sight they would have disappeared anyway because they would no longer be visible because they had shifted out of the third dimension's range.

And they'd arc back round and return to their higher plane. It's... it's unbelievable and yet this is what has been going on for thousands and thousands of years.

So the reason why the craft is saucer-shaped is because the outer-rim of the vortex is a circle emanating from this central point. So if you have a central point and you draw a circle around it you have a saucer or a dish shape.

And the field wasn't flat and therefore the shape of the craft was to mirror the shape of the vortex. That way all of the craft is within the vortex and everything gets shifted.

Scene 7: Interlude 1

THE FILM PAUSES AS THE CAMERA PULLS BACK TO REVEAL MARK SITTING AT HIS DESK IN HIS OFFICE. IT IS NOW 13TH DECEMBER 2022, THE PAUSED DOCUMENTARY IS ON HIS SCREEN AS HE TURNS TO FACE YOU.

Hi, I hope you didn't mind me pausing the documentary at this point. It's been several weeks since I did this filming and I've been spending this time editing the documentary. And I realized that some of the things I'm describing are perhaps quite difficult to visualize and that 3D models would help, for example of Stonehenge.

You've already seen some of these models in the documentary and there are many more to come.

But there's something I wanted to explain. It's quite important, but I couldn't really do so at the beginning but now that you've got more context, now that you understand that there are higher dimensions and that there are beings on higher dimensions, then what I'm going to share with you now will make more sense.

And what it is, I want to go into more detail about how it is I actually get the information, but importantly as well I'd like to give you more of an insight into the process.

When I was about seven years old I started meditating and it was all done naturally and intuitively. In fact I didn't even know the word "Meditation", I was just closing my eyes and "Going inside".

By about the age of twelve I'd had some pretty profound realizations and experiences on the inside and after many... literally thousands and thousands of hours of meditation, and dedication, by 2009 I attained a state, which many people refer to as "Enlightenment".

Chapter 30: Enlightenment

Now the word enlightenment is often used and it means different things to different people so let me explain a little bit more about what I mean when I say enlightenment.

In that final meditation my consciousness transcended all limits going beyond the bounds of time and space and vibration to that great "Oneness" if you like. And my spirit, again transcended the boundaries of everything and returned to "The Source".

Now this physical body and all that you see is no different than it was before that. It's a vehicle for what happens down here.

But it means that from that point on, when I go on the inside, I'm able to have awareness that transcends time, transcends space and for most people that realization of enlightenment, because I'm not the first to do this, that realization is considered "The end of the journey".

But one of the things I understood at that moment was that this was "The beginning" for me and so I continued exploring and learning how to go into that greater state. And because it is beyond time and beyond boundaries and limitations then anything that has ever happened, anything that has ever been known, any event that has ever occurred, is within that greater-state of being.

And as such after many many more years I learnt that I could go inside and get information about what has happened in the past, because from that greater-state, which is beyond time there is no such thing as "The past" and so all knowledge is effectively there. And what I was learning was how to access it.

In the documentary I attempt to give an idea of the state of getting information, but it can't really be represented. The take-home message is that it comes from a state transcending intellectual-awareness and even perception; vastly different from the many lower-realm ways people typical attempt to explore the non-physical dimensions with such as: Mediumship, divination, meditation, remote viewing, astral projection, dowsing, clairaudience, clairvoyance, scrying, 3rd eye, Akashic Records, kundalini, 'letting things in', visualisation, psychotropics, or mind-based work.

Now when I first started doing this I encountered beings on higher dimensions. And just as down here in... on the third dimension, some people are good, some people are not so good, I soon realized that it was the same on higher dimensions as well.

And some of them tried to mislead me and give me false information but I soon realized that was happening and because of this vaster state, which they don't have, I was able to go beyond that limit that they presented and to know the truth.

Anyone who is seeking higher-dimensional awareness is likely to experience similar deceptions by negative beings on higher dimensions. I've produced a free video [1] to help all understand and avoid one of the mainstream ways such dark beings are currently deceiving good spiritual people. That guidance is also covered in the book "Spiritual Life Explained" [2] and you can find links to these at the end of this book.

And so though in the beginning I could interact with these higher-beings and get information from them, some good serving the light, and some trying to mislead me, I soon realized that I didn't need to and I could go beyond even the limits that they knew and know whatever it was that needed to be known.

But it was in discovering these beings on higher dimensions and realizing that "Not all were good" that I came across The Leader and in time discovered the information about his Druids, information that he did not wish me to know.

But having access to knowledge is not the same as knowing how to access it and so the skill that I have learned over many more years is how to have that enquiry.

So this gives you a little bit more of a context and awareness of how it is that I'm able to get information, even if it is ancient and even if it is hidden.

But as I've alluded to the real skill is in accessing it. All this information is like a vast almost endless puzzle. Each fragment of information is a puzzle piece.

You don't simply get all of the knowledge if you want to know something, the skill is in knowing how to pursue it and so you start with an enquiry, and that brings forth a fragment of information.

And then with experience I've learned how to follow the thread and that piece leads to that piece leads to that piece and eventually a bigger picture starts to emerge.

But the information is neutral, it's just there, and so...

"It's the pursuit of truth that matters"

...because truth and light go hand in hand and it is through pursuing truth that light is shed upon the information, to bring it to light.

And sometimes I've been guided by those who serve the light on higher dimensions, who've brought certain bits of information to my attention so that I can look into it further.

One such ascended human was instrumental in helping me learn about the propulsion system used by the interdimensional craft. He had been displeased at the use of dark technology for a long time and so when I started to enquire into it he helped guide me in the right direction. Though I do not name him here, I thank him. You may wonder why I don't name him and the reason is simple: There are many dark beings on higher dimensions who would impersonate him and other good ascended humans. In fact many so called *"Ascended Masters"* or *"Lords"* are nothing more than agents of The Leader, deceiving people on the physical plane who make contact with higher dimensions.

Over the course of many years of doing this I've gathered a mass of information and it's this bigger picture, putting together all these puzzle pieces, that are in the books as well as the... describing the process and the unfolding realizations that have led to this. And the documentary that we're looking at here is but a small fragment of this bigger picture.

So bringing it back to this documentary, when I decided that I was going to make these 3D models, at that point we knew that there were craft that could travel between dimensions. And so in order to make the models I needed to know what they looked like; how many crew were in them; how they were powered; and all of these things. Because truth matters and I wish to represent the truth as accurately as possible.

When I realized having already filmed much that I needed to go inside and bring more information down, it brought up a lot more about the craft. And so what I'd like to invite you to join me in, is we're going to pause this video here and jump forwards in time. Tomorrow I'm going to return to Stonehenge so that I can share this new information that has come about through the process of making these 3D models, about the craft and how they looked and how they functioned in much more detail, and then we'll return to where we are now.

IT IS 4:30 AM 14TH DECEMBER 2022. MARK LOADS THE CAMERA GEAR INTO THE CAMPERVAN.

AS HE SETS OFF FOR STONEHENGE. THE HEADLAMPS OF THE VAN GLARE TURNING THE SCREEN WHITE.

Scene 8: UFOs at Stonehenge

THE WHITE SCREEN FADES TO REVEAL THE VAN PARKED
ALONGSIDE STONEHENGE ON A CRISP, COLD AND FROSTY
MORNING.

*So here we are back at what is quite a sunny day at Stonehenge.
And there it is. It's about minus two (centigrade) today so there's
a few people less than last time we were here.*

Chapter 31:   Showing the Craft: First Try

*But I've come back because as I explained, since I did the last bit
of filming we found out even more information and that draws
our attention to the stones which by now we understand to be an
interdimensional spaceport, like an airport really.*

As you could hear it was an extremely windy day and it was just not possible to carry on filming. I'd have to wait till the following day. So I made the use of the time in the van to do some more editing of this documentary.

Good Morning!

Well another sunny day, It was about... We'll let them go past... It was about minus eight, minus nine last night, but it's a gorgeous sunny day so I think it's time to walk the dog and then we're going to do some filming.

MARK LIFTS HIS DOG OUT THE VAN, TALKING TO HIM

Are you ready? Come on then... To me, let's go... Do you want to go for a walkies? Okay. Good boy.

80

Chapter 32: Showing the Craft: Second Try

I'm back here to talk specifically about the craft so let's recap what we understand so far...

MARK SUDDENLY STOPS SPEAKING, TURNS TO LOOK TO HIS RIGHT AND THE FILM PAUSES.

Well it's never a dull moment it seems at Stonehenge! We're just going to head off now. The police have just come along, they're closing this road and asking everyone to move.

Honestly you couldn't make this up. I was all set up to film and the police arrived! They kindly gave me one hour to wrap up filming. But then there was interference, this time on the audio equipment so I had to abandon filming! Two hours later I returned to the public footpath alongside Stonehenge and set up my tripod and camera. There was no one in shot or nearby as it was freezing cold and late in the day. But as soon as I started filming people started gathering where I was, making filming more challenging. Coincidence or interference? Let's just say the truth is stranger than fiction.

Chapter 33:   Showing the Craft: Third Try

Okay so here we are yet again back at Stonehenge. We had to move location because the police and the council came and closed the entire site.

It was a public road but they shut it down because in a few, well literally, in a week is the winter solstice and they are expecting a lot of people to turn up there, so they've decided to close that road altogether, which is fair enough.

Now we're here specifically to focus on the craft. Let's first recap what we know so far. It creates a vortex so it's got a vortex generator and that allows it to shift in vibration. And it also has the need for very dark and ungodly energy and that's what is used to power it.

Chapter 34:   UFO Flying From Stonehenge

So let's take a closer look, I mean, imagine what would it look like if it was here right now today coming out from the actual Stonehenge as it is today.

It's certainly very golden, that's the first thing you notice.

This shot of the craft in present day Stonehenge is my favourite one. It was actually the first 3D scene I imagined doing. I didn't know how to achieve it but I wanted to visually show you what I'd discovered. So over several months I taught myself 3D modelling and compositing. Now when I see this shot it reminds me of the hard work, but more so the satisfaction that comes from sharing truth.

Now with the craft above us the first thing that really stands out is underneath it there appear to be six thruster-like objects.

This is how the craft was 9,000 BC, 11,000 years ago. Since then there's been a lot of other types of craft and some have more thrusters some have less but this is actually how these... these original craft were with six.

But there's nothing significant about that number in this particular case it's just the way that these craft were built. We'll talk some more about the thrusters in a bit.

Now if the craft were to drop down and lean towards us slightly then we'd be able to see, as you can see now, that there is a domed-windscreen across the top and that too has a golden tint to it.

And we can start to make out within it there is an orb at the top of the windscreen, dead central to the craft, and there is also an orb within the centre of the craft and these are two of the key features that I wanted to discuss with you in more detail.

Chapter 35:   They Like Gold

But first, why is it that the craft and the windscreen are golden? Well the windscreen is actually impregnated with golden-particles all the way throughout its surface.

The craft itself is also coated in gold. Now in the book I talk a lot more about the material and spiritual significance of gold and its role in the bigger picture.

Suffice to say at this stage that the use of gold in this craft is not positive, it is something quite nefarious. And there is no coincidence either that, if you remember back to when *The Leader* was introduced, *The Leader* was shown wearing a gold cloak. Gold is used a lot by the ungodly. But let's go back to the spheres that we could see; let's take a closer look.

Chapter 36:   Vortex Generator

In the centre of this craft, if we zoom right in, we will see the actual vortex generator.

THE CRAFT ZOOMS IN TOWARDS THE CAMERA, ITS OUTER SURFACE DISAPPEARING TO REVEAL A CROSS-SECTION VIEW INSIDE.

Now this is encased in a dodecahedron containment system. This is made out of a very complex metal alloy which has a single leg attached to the base of the craft.

In each of the node points of this dodecahedron is a field emitter and these create a spherical field to contain the vortex emitter.

Chapter 37:   The Vortex Emitter

The vortex emitter itself is that very bright centre, it's called the emitter core and that's at the very centre. And you'll notice that rotating around it are two spheres but they are incomplete and they are made of almost square sheets of a very metallic-alloy, and they are rotating in different directions to each other.

And the gaps in these spheres allow the operators of the craft to regulate the vortex by allowing more or less of the energy to emanate from this core.

Chapter 38:   The Vortex

So that whole system is effectively a containment and regulation system for the vortex emitter which is the bright core at the centre.   And it's from this centre that the vortex is emitted outwards.

And as you can see it arches up round and comes back in. And if you were to look at it from above it would seem almost like a toroid. And though a toroid has a hole in the centre, the way this field works is the entire craft including the centre bit is encased in, almost like the silhouette of the field.

So although it comes back in, it loops around again and creates this overall containment field. And everything within this field is shifted in vibration including the field emitter, the craft, the personnel within, when the vortex is activated, either shifting it up or shifting it down.

Chapter 39:   The Gravity Drive

Now shifting in vibration is one thing, and say the craft was on a higher dimension and they shifted in vibration. They would have changed vibration but they would still be stuck on that higher dimension.

So this craft is nothing without its propulsion system. And so we draw our attention to the orb at the top the one that's in the windshield.

Now I would like to be able to tell you what it's called but the interesting phenomena about how information comes down is that you don't necessarily get the names of things rather you get the nature of them.

So I understand what it is, I understand how it works, but it is a completely different kind of enquiry to be able to get the label or the name that someone else would have used for it in the past. So for this purpose we'll simply call it the "Gravity Drive".

And what that orb is doing is it's creating, just above the craft, a "Gravity well", which we can now see.

Now you wouldn't normally see the gravity well because it's a distortion in the fabric of space, it wouldn't necessarily be visible to your eye, but you can see it there.

And the way it works is this gravity well is like a... you could think of it like a black hole. It's not a black hole but that's probably the easiest way to understand it.

Because it's above the craft the craft falls upwards into the gravity well. But because the well is being emitted by the craft then as the craft falls upwards the well moves as well and so they keep sync with each other and the craft rises.

And they can change the angle that this gravity well is projected at so that they can go upwards and forwards, or backwards or sideways in any direction. And if they want to descend they simply weaken the gravity well and there is less falling upwards *and they then are influenced by the gravity of the environment they are in and they fall down.*

Chapter 40:   Gravity is Density

Now when we talk about gravity the phenomena of gravity certainly does exist. If you were to sit under a tree and an apple fell out, it would hit you on the head.

But the theories and explanations of gravity that we have at this time differ from how these ancient and far more technically-advanced races would understand gravity.

First of all ,they understand the multi-dimensional nature of the fabric of creation. They're not just looking at everything in terms of the physical plane, and they understand that what gravity is is density.

Now we can use the word "Density" in two contexts. There's the density of matter around us and this is why for example a fish will float in water because it is less dense.

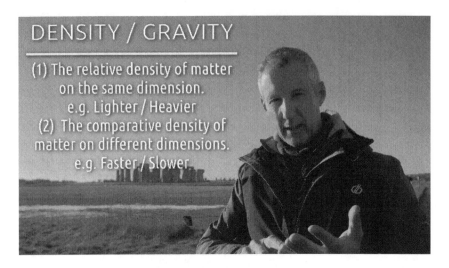

DENSITY / GRAVITY

(1) The relative density of matter on the same dimension.
e.g. Lighter / Heavier
(2) The comparative density of matter on different dimensions.
e.g. Faster / Slower

A submarine can rise or sink in the water by changing its density by filling its ballast tanks with water or purging them of water and so by changing the density of an object it can rise or fall in water.

That's also from a higher perspective why we land on the ground and why Stonehenge stays on the ground, because it's at the same density as the ground.

If you took the stones up into the air they would be much denser than the air and they would fall towards the more dense part of creation and it's the same on all dimensions.

So gravity does exist but it's perceived as density not some kind of weak hard-to-prove attractive force.

It simply is that when the craft creates this gravity well above it it's creating a denser place than the surrounding and the craft, being dense, will attract to that density; it falls into it.

So this gravity engine is the main propulsion system of the craft and it's capable of allowing the craft to traverse the entire diameter of the physical plane in minutes, but what it's not very good at is finesse.

This is a brute-force drive and if you were to rely on this gravity well, this attachment if you like to a gravity field, and try and land you'd probably crash, and historically there are some examples of things going wrong.

To try and imagine why that would be: If you had a very heavy weight on the end of a bungee cord and you were swinging that bungee cord around, your hand would be the gravity well and wherever you swing it the heavy weight would be the craft.

And it would be fine for making it move rapidly and then the elastic nature of the bungee cord would cause the craft to overcompensate. And so when you watch these craft they're always in a state of movement, because they're constantly falling into the gravity well and having to make adjustments. If they

95

want to stay in one place then they have to fall and then ease off the strength of the well to drop back and so they can't easily stay in one place.

And so manoeuvring down to land the craft on the ground just isn't possible, you'd end up crashing, as has happened.

Chapter 41:   The Thrusters

And so they devised the system of thrusters and the thrusters' job is primarily to decelerate as they come into land and control the fine movements to gently land the craft. And then to take the craft off before the gravity well takes over and they rapidly move away.

When we talk about thrusters, like me, you're probably thinking: "Was it solid fuel or liquid fuel? Some kind of maybe electric drive or something?"   When I did the work to go inside and bring down the knowledge of how the thrusters worked, I've got to be honest this was something that really surprised me, and not in a good way either!

The first thing to consider or to understand is that energy on a much higher dimension, as I've said, should not be down here and when it does come down here it's much stronger. It's like it's potentized by coming down here.

The second thing to understand is that emotions... and you may be wondering where I'm going with this, stick with me. Emotions are fundamentally a basic thought, not an intellectual thought but a basic thought.

And that thought would be for example "I like" in which case there's a lot of positive feelings and emotion about attraction towards something. Or you might have the emotion of "I dislike" in which case there's a repulsion, a sense of wanting to move away from something.

And all emotions are fundamentally a thought with energy. Negative emotions like anger or hate tend to have negative energy and positive emotions tend to have positive energy.

But what they realized a long time ago is if they made some really really evil dark energy, something that should not exist, and they made it on a really high dimension and then brought it down to this dimension, it would become a powerful force.

And then if they used it as emotional energy then the thought within that emotion for example "Repulsion" would direct the energy, because energy alone doesn't act, it needs a thought to compel it if you like.

And so what these thrusters are, those balls that we see, are actually balls of highly-disgusting, evil, dark energy...

...compressed, and within each one they've been imbued with an abject thought of core basic repulsion.

And so as the craft is coming in the pilot can manipulate the amount of that emotional energy to cause repulsion. And so it's these drives pushing against their environment, literally the energy and the thought of "Repulsion" from higher dimensions having a massive effect on the third dimension to effectively hold up this craft and allow it to be gently lowered to the ground.

You could say it's pure genius but it's also pure evil and darkness.

And so if this sounds crazy I assure you you've probably already heard of this very principle. See anytime a picture falls off a wall, or an object flies across a room, or a door slams, in what people quite often term "Poltergeist activity" or when there's a "Presence" in a house, that's "Psychokinesis".

It's an emotional outburst causing movement of physical matter. That's what psychokinesis means, and these thrusters are actually "Psychokinetic-thrusters". They're using an abominable energy with a really intense negative emotion to thrust against the environment, literally repulsing everything around them.

And if you were here with me right now in close vicinity to this craft you would probably experience a coppery, almost acidic, taste on your tongue, and you might even feel a tingling in your, in your crown chakra in the back of your head.

Some people might even notice a very unpleasant pungent smell and what this is, is the negative energy coming off that craft is being sensed. Because it's not a chemical it's an emotion it's picked up by your aura and your system is trying to make sense of it.

And it literally, if you're in the vicinity of something like this, the negativity coming off it will be experienced by you as taste or smell or sensations that are all letting you know "This is really unpleasant you need to move away".

So with its psychokinetic-thrusters and its a anti-gravity system using a gravity well and a gravity drive, and its interdimensional vortex generator. This craft is able to move between dimensions, *to manipulate itself and manoeuvre itself on the physical plane, as well as on higher-planes, and to move at phenomenal speeds.*

And it's understandable knowing all of this, especially if you're scientifically minded, that you'd be wondering if this could be replicated?

Chapter 42:   Dark Technology?

And certainly in cutting-edge fields right now some of the technology that's involved in this craft is being explored. It might not be in reference to making an interdimensional craft but people are already looking at wormholes, quantum tunnelling, quantum computing, particle accelerators and all of these things.

And by the way I appreciate this is totally often well intended.

And then in the fringe fields people are looking at free-energy devices trying to tap into the mysterious "Black matter" or "Antimatter" that makes up the bulk of the cosmos; or trying to create "Zero points" to draw down or manifest energy.

With the understanding of the multi-dimensional nature of creation I can tell you, all of these activities, no matter how positive the intentions behind them are, no matter how good the people doing the research are; I'm not questioning their goodness or their, their motivation; but all of these scientific endeavours are fundamentally ungodly.

Because what they are doing is they are disturbing, breaking, or distorting the fabric of creation, the dimensional-fabric, to bring energy down that should not be here, or to create energy that should not exist. And this is exactly what these dark and evil beings figured out literally eighteen thousand years ago at Atlantis and they've been refining it ever since. And whether it is that we are being manipulated as a society to bring these technologies to the third dimension at this time, or whether we're getting there by our own scientific prowess is irrelevant. What we are discovering is ancient and it should not exist. And on higher dimensions I can tell you this much:

*"Those that serve the light
do not use technology."*

103

THOSE THAT SERVE THE LIGHT DO NOT USE TECHNOLOGY

There is no such thing as good technology. Craft are not meant to manipulate their environment and travel between dimensions.

And that energy I talked about that they created on higher dimensions to be able to create these balls of intense negativity and evil and darkness to use as thrusters; that should not exist.

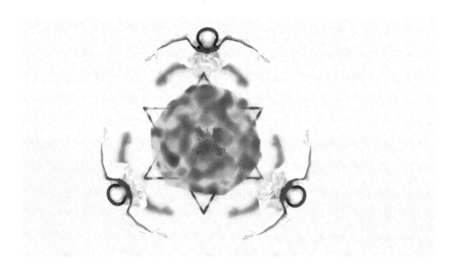

And so the work of these ungodly beings isn't just an abomination on the third dimension, it's an abomination on every single dimension.

And whether we're doing it blindly or being guided, society is moving in that direction and so it has to be said "We need to stop!".

> *"Just because something can be done,
> doesn't mean that it should be done."*

And those that serve the light on higher dimensions have made it very clear that:

> *"They do not wish to see this technology
> being developed on the third dimension."*

So "Yes" this craft is fascinating, but the purpose for it must not be forgotten and the ones who created it must not be forgotten and they all are using these craft to come down here and to control YOU.

They've been manipulating society for thousands of years. I do not believe it is a coincidence that we are now replicating, or starting to learn how to replicate, the technology that they have been using to enslave us all this time.

THE DOCUMENTARY PAUSES AND THE CAMERA PULLS BACK REVEALING THE FOOTAGE ON THE SCREEN IN MARK'S OFFICE. IT IS NOW THE 20TH DECEMBER 2022 AND MARK TURNS AWAY FROM THE SCREEN TO FACE YOU.

Scene 9: Interlude 2

Welcome back. Well that was certainly fascinating and it really gives an insight into how so much of what we maybe believe to be cutting-edge technology in our present day, could actually have its roots not only in the ancient past but perhaps even on higher dimensions.

But let us return now to where we left off. The story at Stonehenge isn't quite finished and after Stonehenge I'm going to invite you to join me as we take a journey to Avebury, where there are even more revelations and insights. Not only into our ancient past but also into how things are the way they are in the present day.

THE FILM RESUMES AT THE POINT WHERE IT PAUSED FOR INTERLUDE 1. RETURNING TO 15TH NOVEMBER 2022 .

Scene 10: Stonehenge Revisited #2

Now you could actually touch the craft but you would have had to enter into that perimeter and you would have probably suffered quite badly from radiation.

The occupants of the craft however, they could come out and because they were of a higher-di(mensional)... of a higher-vibration, they were from higher dimensions, their bodies and their form are meant to be exposed to higher-vibrational-energy and so they didn't suffer any ill effect from the vibration, from the radiation.

Chapter 43: Non-Physical Visitors

And they could come out leave the craft walk out of the kind of safety perimeter of the sarsen stone circle and then meet with the Druids.

And that's exactly what would happen.

Now they would have about ten hours from when they landed to when they had to leave for two reasons. Maintaining the vortex on the craft took a lot of energy so ten hours is about the maximum. And once they stepped out of that vortex field that

was suppressing their vibration to drop it down to pseudo-physical third-dimensional-vibration they would start the process of returning to their own vibration.

Now it wouldn't happen instantly but if they stayed outside that field for more than ten hours they would just start to fade.

Now remember they're not actually made of physical matter they're made of energy and matter on higher dimensions, their matter would start to return to its natural vibration and if you were standing... say I, you know... say this is one of them, then they would just fade away.

They wouldn't actually be gone but you would no longer be able to perceive them, but they would now be in a bit of bother because they'd be stuck on this plane but at the wrong vibration.

Chapter 44:   Ten Hour Time Limit

So they had a maximum of ten hours and often they wouldn't stay even half of that. But they would do their work, talk about what needed to be done: Go and attack that village, this person has to leave the group, design this technology, whatever the... the... the... instruction was.

And obviously they were always teaching them about magic and things like this because a lot of the suppression is to do with thought and a lot of the black magic they were doing and the... the circles and the stones and the work they did in nature was to actually set up negative energy grids around the planet.

For the next 3,000 years these biannual meetings carried on, visitors came down and then again things were evolving on higher dimensions, and The Leader and those really close to him like Pan, over this time they hadn't been standing still.

Humanity was now evolving. We're coming up to about 6,000 BC and you've got the rise of the Egyptian cities and Mesopotamia and this was because three of those races that had been involved with this Druid council had broken ranks and set up their own cities in defiance of The Leader.

They had gained power on higher dimensions as well, suddenly there was much more conflict between these ruling races on

111

higher dimensions, and there had always been conflict between many of the other races, of which there are many.

Earth was the prize, and in this pursuit of governance and rule The Leader had developed a vast array of knowledge, all of which was dark: Black magic, mind control, thought control, manipulation, technologies and energies that should never have existed.

Knowledge was power and it still is to this day, which is why these dark forces do not want you to know the truth about things like Stonehenge or the truth about higher dimensions.

But even back then, 6,000 BC, The Leader was facing a rapidly changing situation on the planet. Other races were starting in defiance, to come down and had their own agendas and plans for humanity on this planet, on this physical plane.

What he prized most and what gave him his edge was he was seen as "The master of all that is dark" and so he needed somewhere to hide his knowledge.

But understand this, humanity are good. Our birthright is light.

*And there are forces for good far greater than even this leader and all those who are dark and evil work in the shadows. The thing they fear more than absolutely anything is the truth of what they are doing being brought **into the light.***

And so they have to hide in secrecy, even if they hide in plain sight amongst us today.

And so he needed somewhere where he could hide his dark knowledge, not only from his enemies and the other races and groups, and even from some of his own ranks. But from the light.

And he took all of his knowledge and his understanding of the third dimension and bearing in mind that the third dimension itself was under a dark firmament, which is why we're so kept in the dark about higher dimensions and the source of light. But he took all of this knowledge and he realized that Stonehenge presented a wonderful opportunity.

You see what he needed was a library, somewhere he could archive off all of his knowledge and then when he was training his acolytes he could send them to this secret library and in secret they could gain the knowledge that he wanted them to have.

And this brings us on to Avebury, and it's at Avebury that we will find this library.

Scene 11: The Journey to Avebury

WE ARE NOW IN THE CAMPERVAN LOOKING THROUGH THE
FRONT WINDSCREEN, MARK DRIVING, BLUE ON THE
PASSENGER SEAT, WATCHING THE SCENERY FLY PAST IN A
TIMELAPSE.

*Join me as we head north to Avebury, a straight line journey
of just over 17 miles. There's much more to discover there
but first let's recap what we now know.*

*About 9,700 BC a being of immense evil from higher
dimensions instructed his agents on the third dimension,
known as Druids, to make a giant year clock.*

BC 9,700 the Leader
asks his druids to make
the "Year clock"

*Twice a year he came down to them by interdimensional
tunnel fuelled by black magic and ungodly energy. As well as
putting in place dark magic and energy grids they also
interfered and meddled with affairs on Earth in order to
mislead and enslave humanity.*

700 years later he gave them technology to move giant stones and they created the stone circles to facilitate interdimensional craft first seen on Atlantis thousands of years before.

By BC 6,000 some of his allies had turned against him and other groups were interested in manipulating humanity and so to keep his advantage he sought to hide his evil knowledge in a library on the third dimension. Thus the Avebury site was formed.

Across this vast expanse of time this leader and the other dark and evil races have all had a single goal: To prevent you from discovering your true nature as a being of light and to stop you reaching for the source of that light.

They want to keep you in the dark, and technology is the key to their success.

Scene 12: Avebury

So we've just arrived at the southernmost part of the Avebury site and these stones, one here and the one behind me, represent the entrance to what is a long gateway that you can see going off heading north to the stone circle.

And we're going to walk, it's about one kilometre, and at the other end we should find the southern edge of the stone circle.

Now these stones were brought here in exactly the same way as the Druids used technology to move the stones at Stonehenge.

Now as we walk up here it's about kilometre (good boy) and it will obviously take me quite a few minutes. And you saw the drive on the way here as well and that was obviously not as direct a route because we had to go around the roads but even thousands of years ago when there were no roads it would have still been quite a trek.

Now you remember me saying that those visitors from higher dimensions only had a maximum of really of ten hours and when I said that they created a library at Avebury, obviously they had to get there.

Chapter 45: From Stonehenge to Avebury?

Now they couldn't use the craft because the energy demands just to keep the craft at this dimension, at this vibration, were quite high. It was purely there to get them here and to take them home, so they had to make their way to Avebury.

At the speed I'm going it would have taken them the best part of half of that time. They wouldn't have really had the time to walk all the way here, do what they need to do and then walk back.

The answer to this may be surprising as "How did they do it then?". They didn't have any fancy technology, hover-boards, they didn't use horses.

Because they were higher-dimensional beings and because they had come down into what I call "Pseudo-physicality", although yes they were physical and you could interact with them, they didn't exist in the same physical way that you and I do. They were still fundamentally higher-vibration.

For them there was no weight really, there was no strain and they could literally run super-fast because there was no effect upon them from the... that you and I would experience.

They didn't fatigue, they simply left the craft, had a quick sprint up here and arrived minutes later, did what they need to do and then sprinted back to the craft all with ample of time.

You see things on higher dimensions don't obey the laws of physics as we do and they, although could interact with physical things and though they could be seen, they were not truly physical they were just temporarily physical.

WE ARRIVE AT THE END OF THE AVENUE OF STONES AND SEE A PATH IN THE TREES WHERE THE WALL OF THE HENGE IS VISIBLE.

Chapter 46: Arriving at the Henge

So we're now arriving at the ring of the henge around Avebury, and as you come over this henge you can see the stones.

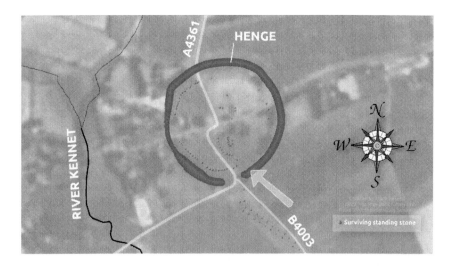

This Village wouldn't have been here in the past and this road through the middle, so you can kind of see a ring of stones and again significantly big. And as before it's the same technology, exactly the same as Stonehenge and that would later be used for the pyramids.

It probably would have been quite something to have seen these circles and the outer-henge when they were first erected. But now that there's this village in the middle of it, traffic driving past and trees growing up around it and within it, it's hard to get an idea of what it might have been.

B lue my dog, is a blue merle collie who I rescued as a young pup and he's grown to be an amazing dog. He's always by my side and is extremely sensitive to energy and things "*Unseen*". I trust his instincts and have learnt to pay close attention when he is unsettled. When we got to Avebury he really started to react and was scared of the stones, or more precisely, what was in and around them. He was on edge all the time I was filming until near the end. You may be able to guess at which point he relaxed as you read on.

If viewed from above you have one giant outer circle, the henge, and then you have two inner circles and buried beneath the ground is also a rectangle, all made of stone.

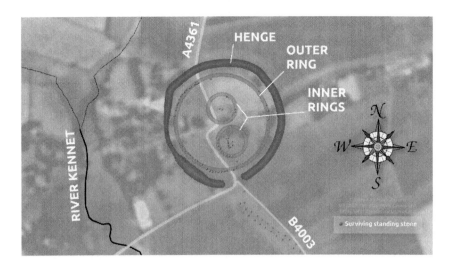

This is quite an impressive stone. I'm six foot tall and I come about yay high, so I'm guessing this is at least ten foot above the ground. Wider at the top so there's no way it landed there according to nature.

Okay this stone behind me is just one of the many stones at the Avebury site forming two inner-rings and then the outer-ring. The inner-rings are the library as are the buried stones forming a rectangle.

Chapter 47: The Dark Library

When I said "Library" you may have been forgiven for thinking in terms of paper, ink, and books and ironically just over there is a second-hand bookshop.

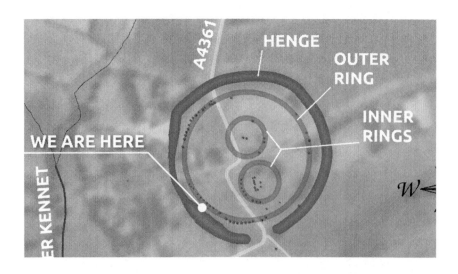

But these are multi-dimensional beings from a higher dimension. They don't work in terms of ink and paper, for them it's all about thought so they needed a library of thought.

And it turns out that the third dimension has something very very special, it has silica and in particular quartz. Now all these rocks contain, even if it's just microscopic, they contain quartz crystals and it turns out that quartz is perfect for storing thought.

And if you talk to people who study crystals they'll talk about programming crystals through intention. Intention is thought and the crystals are able to trap data just as you would put information onto a USB stick. Each one of these stones is actually a repository of thought and therefore information.

124

Now just as in a bookshop or in a library you would find different books on different subjects that's what this is. Each stone covers a separate topic.

Now all the topics were concerned with things like dark magic, mind control, technology, basically things to do with suppressing humanity, controlling humanity, or general wrongdoing.

Chapter 48:   Writing the Library Books

And you may wonder, well how did the information get into the stones? It's very simple, it started with The Leader. He would come down.

> THE LEADER ENTERS THE SHOT FROM THE LEFT AND APPROACHES THE STONE, STANDING IN FRONT OF IT.

He would telepathically transmit the information he wanted into the stone and then he would use an array of dark magic, invocations, and incantations, and spells to protect that information. That stone now locked in place with its knowledge.

Only someone that had the right incantations and invocations would be able to access that information. In time not just The Leader but those close to him such as Pan also came down and imbued their knowledge into specific stones. And thus a library of dark and evil knowledge was embedded into the physical matter at Avebury.

Once the information was there it was very straightforward for those who The Leader intended, his acolytes those he was training in the dark arts, to come here and access that information.

He would say to them "Take the next craft down at solstice and go to stone number four, stone number seven, and stone number fourteen" for example and he would give them the incantation to unlock each of the stones.

Chapter 49: Accessing the Library

They would sit in front of the stone, using telepathy they would do the incantation, which would unlock the knowledge. And then they would telepathically draw it to them and they would then know, at a thought-level, the knowledge of that stone.

It was clever because in this way The Leader made sure that only the information he wanted could be accessed by that person. Otherwise if it wasn't for the protection in place someone could come and they could gather all of the knowledge, and since knowledge is power they would then be able to challenge The Leader.

So The Leader kept the keys. He knew the incantations the invocations necessary, no one else did, and that way he could train his students in the dark arts, but only... each one only had a small piece of the overall picture. They knew enough to do what he wanted them to do, but not to challenge him.

Chapter 50:   Hidden From the Light

Now the protection wasn't just about protecting the knowledge in each stone, remember he hid the knowledge down here on the third dimension plane to keep it out of the light.

And so the outer henge that's running behind us here and round there and the stones around the perimeter acted as an anchor point for energy grid, a dome, covering the entire site shrouding it in darkness and therefore keeping the light out.

So this monumental construction is far from a sacred site. It is something far far more nefarious, probably one of the most condensed repositories of ungodly and evil energy, thought, knowledge, which has been used since 6,000 BC when this was constructed to suppress humanity, to keep us literally in the dark.

When I finished filming I was really saddened at the thought
of all the evil and darkness that had been put into this land.
I felt compelled to bless the ground and declare, as one who
serves the light, that the forces of darkness
could no longer claim this place.

When I looked up there was that wonderful rainbow, which I
just showed, and I knew there was nothing left to do or say
here. What needed to be brought to light has been
and it was time to leave.

The unexpected sunshine which had allowed me to film
receded and sure enough just as I made it to the van
the rains came down with poetic timing.

Scene 13: Leaving Avebury

WE FIND OURSELVES IN THE CAB OF THE CAMPERVAN, THE ENGINE RUNNING AS MARK PREPARES TO DRIVE OFF. RAIN RUNS DOWN THE WINDOWS.

Well it looks like we're leaving Avebury just in time. Literally just as I got to the van and sat down the rain came. We were blessed there with the weather, to actually be able to do some filming and not get completely soaked through.

So we're for the last time going to head back to the Stonehenge Campsite. Perhaps it's fitting though as we leave Avebury behind us that we talk about the the downfall or the end of Stonehenge and the Druids.

Chapter 51:   Stonehenge's Demise

The library at Avebury and indeed the airport at Stonehenge served The Leader well, but there is one constant and that is change. And by 6,000 BC some of the races that had been allied with The Leader, in particular the ones that are very technologically advanced, and other races, were starting to come down and make their own colonies and bases on Earth, on the third dimension.

And those ones that broke rank from his alliance, he would in time attack their cities with his own armies.

I wonder how many people watching the film failed to notice the Egyptian pyramids seen through the side window as I said "*He would attack their cities*". You can see one in the previous image. This hints that some historical battles, such as when Egypt was attacked in ancient times, were orchestrated by different races on higher-dimensions, fighting for control over the third dimension. You might therefore want to consider if modern day conflicts are also influenced by similar dark groups?

But he was losing control in some respects and so by about 6,000 BC things were changing and things had to evolve from his point of view as well. Technology was also changing.

So by 400 BC the site at Stonehenge no longer had significance to him, he'd built up a large presence in South America and was influencing the civilizations there, building a power base.

The technology had changed as well and there were more energy-efficient, less energy-consuming ways of bringing people down to the third dimension and returning them to higher dimensions.

They still used the vortex technology to shift vibration.

But the propulsion was something much more similar to what you might recognize as aircraft today. And indeed the craft that were developed around about 400 BC look a lot like the craft of today. And there are actually statues and amulets and things depicting what looked like aeroplanes that have been found dating back to that period in South America.

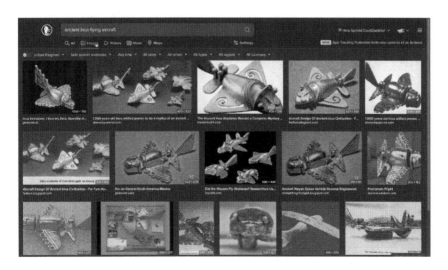

So this brings us to the time of the Nazca Lines. Stonehenge was no longer relevant and we'll talk about what happened to Stonehenge and the Druids in a moment. But he moved his base of operations over to Peru, to the Nazca region.

Chapter 52: The Nazca Lines

And when you look at the lines, it's just an evolution of what he had done at Stonehenge. Using these new craft, which effectively flew rather than were propelled in the way that the saucers were, he built long runways for them to land.

And even today's modern technology marvels at how it could have been possible for him to have these seven-mile long straight lines. It's simple, he used what we would understand to be laser technology to create these long straight lines and then just manual labour to clear the terrain.

So that when you look at the Nazca Lines there's three different structures that you see: There are long straight parallel tracks which are the landing strips literally, the runways. Then there are animal glyphs, and remember back to the constellations, these animal glyphs, which are massive, represent the different races that he granted permission to use his runways. The bigger the glyph the more important that race was in the alliance.

And then the last of the structures that you see at Nazca are these massive geometric mandalas.

- The rain is really coming down!

And these geometric mandalas are in effect the same as the stones that surround the perimeter of Stonehenge or Avebury. They're complex geometries into which are embedded black magic forming large structures of energy and grids of energy over the region.

They also act as anchor points for black magic, effectively anchor points for where the interdimensional tunnels would open so that these craft from higher dimensions could come through into the third dimension plane. So you simply have runways, flags effectively showing who's allowed, and black magic icons and that's it. That's what the Nazca structures and lines are.

And so by 400 BC he retired Stonehenge. Round about then was the last time that any interdimensional craft came down specifically to use Stonehenge and Avebury.

Note, other races have since come down to Stonehenge, attracted by dark energy.

And what happened to The Druids? They're just the lowest-rung of the ladder. Amazingly despite 9,000 years of investment The Leader didn't tell them, he just stopped coming. He stopped sending his envoys and so with no one coming down the Druids didn't know what had happened.

They simply followed orders. Every solstice they gathered in the hope that someone would arrive. They didn't know that things had changed; they were out of communication not knowing what to do they just carried on doing what they had always done, what had been passed down for thousands of years.

And so over the next few hundreds of years and indeed thousands of years until quite recently, they passed down the Druid lore, the Druid knowledge that you "Gather at the solstice to receive instruction", to be... to meet with "The men who come from the stars". It's quite a sad state of affairs, Stonehenge fell into ruin.

The true meaning behind gathering at the solstice got lost as it was passed down from generation to generation, and eventually it was just simply the lore of magic and the symbology of the stones. But there's more to it.

Chapter 53:   A Beacon of Deception

The Leader didn't want those left behind to remember, he made sure that the key bits of information were hidden in their minds. And remember it's all about deception, it's all about "Smoke and mirrors", what a wonderful opportunity Stonehenge now represented to him.

People would come, people would gather, people would ask questions, and people looking for the truth would find Stonehenge in the years and the decades and the centuries to come. And so he left it as a beacon of deception.

When people came they still gathered at the solstice only now they didn't know why. But the legends about healing energy, which remember only really applies to those who are dark, and the legends about involvement with the stars and higher knowledge and beings and things was enough to bring people along.

And so as well as the ancestors of the Druids and the bloodlines of these twelve races that continued, good people would come along.

Chapter 54:   Ungodly Energy

And so what The Leader did was, each solstice he would open up the tunnel, the interdimensional tunnel, and he would release that ungodly energy into that site.

Those people who were drawn to it because they were dark and negative would feel fantastic, they would feel uplifted, and so legend of the healing powers of the stones and of that place and a feeling of awe would continue.

But for those who were good, who had light within them, humanity, they wouldn't necessarily feel sick, but they would be open to mind control and suggestion and subliminal message.

Chapter 55:   Negative Influence

And so as well as sending the energy, which would kind of activate the lower-animal-parts of people, making them feel good, a bit like a drug makes people feel good so that they want more.

The Leader would use the opportunity that any good humans that were there would be, especially if they went into the ritual of dance and taking certain herbs and things, would be easy prey to distract them from the truth by putting thoughts and ideas into them to attract them to the dark arts.

So that they would grow in their interest in things like geometry, magic, symbolism, chanting, witchcraft and all of these things.

It doesn't mean that the intention of the people there was bad and quite often they had good intentions: To heal. "The road to ruin his paved with good intentions" as they say.

And good people, people who... whose birthright is the light, have a natural inner-yearning for something higher, but stuck under that dark firmament, it's like they've been cut off.

And so they would go perhaps to Stonehenge, gather at the solstice, with good intentions and The Leader would prey on them, corrupt their minds, fill them with ideas, to tempt them into things that would take them away from the light.

It doesn't mean that they were bad, it's just that people don't understand what's behind a lot of these things. And even if something feels good, even if something might have some kind of positive outcome in the short-term people don't always understand the cost.

Yes your body can be healed with certain practices but not all healing is good, and what if the cost to gain something on the physical realm is to shut down something, your soul or your spirit, on higher dimensions?

And this is what The Leader and the Druids are working towards, to keep humanity in the dark. And so though he left Stonehenge to rack and ruin, he didn't leave its legacy.

He made sure that it would carry on acting as something that beguiles people, that leads them astray, because of the awe and wonder of this monument.

And it's the same at Avebury, even today as I approached some of the stones there were people deep in devotion with their hands and their forehead pressed against the stone.

Perhaps they were there for healing, or for power, or for some kind of sacred ceremony? But they have no idea of the darkness and the evil that created those stones and what is locked within them. But more on that because the story of the stones and Stonehenge has changed in recent years and I'll talk about that towards the end.

If only people knew the truth and so I know that so many good people go to Stonehenge and Avebury with the best of intentions and quite often come away feeling good.

In the book I'll talk more about the origin of feelings. All I can say at this stage is:

145

"Do not let feelings be your guide."

How you feel is one of the easiest things for those on higher dimensions to manipulate. We're all too easily led by our feelings.

The path of light, the path of the truth, is a much higher path than the seeking of feeling good or even bliss. Even bliss itself is a dead end for the Seeker of Truth.

There's no denying that Stonehenge, Avebury, the Nazca Lines, the pyramids, there's no denying that they're awe-inspiring but they don't come close to the truth that can be revealed when we look beyond this physical realm.

It's this truth, this greater truth, which is your birthright as a human being that The Leader, his Druids, and the councils on all dimensions desperately want you to stay ignorant about.

FADE TO WHITE AS MARK CONTINUES ON THE JOURNEY.

146

Scene 14: Full Circle

WE HAVE JUMPED FORWARD IN TIME TO 15TH DECEMBER 2022 AND WE ARE BACK ON-SITE AT STONEHENGE. IT IS MINUS SIX CENTIGRADE, A CRISP SUNNY DAY.

So here we are back where it all began, the documentary started here and we're nearly at the end, but the story of Stonehenge and Avebury are not actually finished yet. I'll tell you how they end shortly.

Chapter 56:   This is All About You

*I've touched on a number of things including beings from other dimensions, interdimensional craft, magic and all of these things are actually just a small fragment of a much much bigger picture **and this bigger picture is all about <u>YOU</u>.***

My own interest in Stonehenge only came about because I found out who was behind it, who founded the Druids, and it was this leader who's behind so many other things, things that even now shape your life.

And he has always had one purpose, one goal, as far as you are concerned, and that is to keep you in the dark about your birthright. Your birthright is the light and he doesn't want you, as a human being, to know the truth and it was in pursuit of spiritual truth that I discovered who he was and that led me to investigating more about Stonehenge.

This truth that The Leader wants to keep you in the dark about is about your spiritual birthright and this is what I've been researching tirelessly for a long long time and that's what led me to The Leader and that's what ultimately led me here to Stonehenge.

Chapter 57:   An Even Bigger Picture

And in the books that I'm writing I go into a lot of detail about this bigger picture talking much more about the positive and the spiritual-side of things, What really is on higher dimensions and how this all relates to you.

The books that I'm writing aren't being written so that I can profit from them. When they're finally published they're going to be published at a not-for-profit price so that they are as accessible to as many people as possible.

On my website [3] all that I've done, the podcasts, the videos, the articles, it's freely available. I don't charge anything, I don't even ask people to subscribe.

I just want to get the truth out there and like many others who serve the light we're trying to let people know about how much they are in the dark.

I don't want you to just believe what I'm saying, I want you to be inspired by this documentary, just as Stonehenge is inspiring to so many people. I want you to be inspired to ask questions to start to find out more for yourself.

It's all about choice but we can't make choices unless we learn and understand what the choices are.

Chapter 58: The Conclusion to The Story

As I said the story of Stonehenge and Avebury is not yet finished. You may be wondering what happened to the black magic that they imbued into these stones and the dark and esoteric knowledge hidden at Avebury and also the interdimensional tunnel that came from over that way.

Because of the diligence and hard work of those that serve the light, not just on this dimension but on other dimensions, all of these things have been destroyed.

Once they became known they could be dealt with and so all of that hidden knowledge, the black magic, even the ungodly energy has all been removed and so what we're looking at here are just inert stone and the same is true of Avebury and the other sites around the world.

This doesn't mean that those that would do this kind of thing have been completely dealt with and are no more. On higher dimensions The Leader and others still exist and still interfere and meddle in the affairs of the third dimension. They've had thousands of years to lay the groundwork and to put in place organisations and infrastructure.

When talking about dark organisations & infrastructure, I'm not just referring to higher dimensions. You could look at the world around you and simply ask *"Does that person or group serve the light or do they serve darkness?"*

But now that these things are known about and I don't just mean down here, then they can be more easily dealt with and overcome. And the truth is that right now as a human being you have probably never been so free, what remains is to decide what do you want to do with this freedom?

Scene 15: Final Reflections and Thoughts

Firstly I'd like to say thank you for watching this documentary. We're back in the campsite near Stonehenge.

And as you can see the sun is setting.

I was just talking to the owner of the campsite and he asked me what I've been doing and I said "I've been filming a documentary" and naturally he asked "Well what's the documentary about?". I'll leave you to answer that. What have you taken from this documentary? What do you think this is about? Because it's all about what it means to you.

Chapter 59:   Modern Druids?

But there's one last thing. In a week's time a whole load of people are going to descend on Stonehenge and many of them will identify as being Druids. Probably most of them have no idea about The Leader or the information I've shared with you in this video. What I need to really make clear, the word "Druid", and this word has evolved in its pronunciation, now covers a much wider spectrum than what I'm referring to when I talk about the original Druids.

For example, and again I talk about this in the book, in Lindisfarne 2,000 years ago there were wonderful, intelligent, kind people who lived in harmony with nature and they would have been known as Druids.

In other places there were people who identified as Druid because "Druid" eventually became a word synonymous with anyone who is intelligent, who gathers knowledge, who has wisdom, in other words it could be "Wise old man".

Chapter 60:   Your Choice

And so the word "Druid" now does not mean what I was referring to in the past and I wanted to make that clear because whatever people's beliefs are it fundamentally comes down to...

"Do you pursue the Light?
or
Do you pursue Darkness?"

And so that choice, between light and dark, is a choice for everyone. **It's a choice for YOU right now***, so whatever you identify with, whether you consider yourself "Spiritual" or not, whether you consider yourself "A Druid" or not, these are just labels.*

Only you can really know what's in your heart and if anything I hope all I've done is made you aware that there may be choices that have yet to be made. It's a wake-up call to understand the ancient history behind these things.

Is it more important to identify as "A Druid" or is it more important to connect inside with LIGHT, with LOVE with the source of all of them, that great ONENESS that goes by other names?

That's really what this is about.

PEACE be with you.

Appendix

Links to External Resources

[1] **Video & Article:** *Warning About Abraham and "The Secret"*

thewaybackgroup.org/articles/abrahams-dark-secret/

[2] **Book:** *Spiritual Life Explained: The Wake-up Call*

thewaybackgroup.org/articles/book-spiritual-life-explained/

[3] **Website:** *Free spiritual articles, eBooks, podcasts, & videos*

thewaybackgroup.org

Free Resources Related to This Book

You will find links to watch the original documentary online and download

the audio book version for free at: zaretti.com/stonehenge

Listen to the original documentary audiobook in 5 parts:

Available on all good podcast directories including Spotify, Apple, etcetera.

Simply search for "TWB - Spiritual Audio books".

A Creative Work

All text, footage, 3D models, graphics and artwork are original works of art by
Mark P Zaretti. Any likeness of the 3D modelled characters to real persons is
purely coincidental. The "*Spiritual*" information shared in the documentary and
this book comes from non-physical sources and is provided '*as is*', under the
context of reportage and education, in the spirit of openly sharing knowledge.
Public domain (CC) image attribution: Pyramids: https://pxhere.com/en/photo/821492

The Third Reason

I promised I would explain the third reason why I made this book adaptation of the film. Recently I produced a mini-series of four podcasts about spiritual life, which was so popular I compiled them into a book called "Spiritual Life Explained: The Wake-up Call", which debuted in the Amazon Best Sellers top 50.

A week after that book was published I was hosting a spiritual group meetup and several participants commented on just how much they had got from reading that book. I asked them to tell me which parts had really helped and they gave examples.

Now here is the interesting thing. All these people had recently listened to the podcasts, but it seems that they had completely missed some parts of the podcast! Yet those same parts, word for word, had really resonated with them when they had read the book.

One person even struggled to believe that what they had read in the book was also in the podcast, they had not heard it at all despite giving the podcast their attention. It shows just how positively-powerful reading a book can be.

I guess there are many reasons why people get a lot more from books compared to video or audio. For example, they can read it at their own pace. But I suspect one of the strongest reasons is that when you listen to a podcast or video, it is someone else's voice you hear on the outside, whereas when you read a book to yourself, it is your voice you hear on the inside.

Reading a book is a very intimate, impactful, and precious experience and this is the third reason why I undertook the work to produce this book. I truly hope it has helped you.

God bless you, Mark.

Printed in France by Amazon
Brétigny-sur-Orge, FR

15834862R00094